MEGAN RAPINOE
Making a Difference as an Athlete

By Katie Kawa

KidHaven
PUBLISHING

Published in 2021 by
KidHaven Publishing, an Imprint of Greenhaven Publishing, LLC
353 3rd Avenue
Suite 255
New York, NY 10010

Designer: Deanna Paternostro
Editor: Katie Kawa

Photo credits: Cover Marcio Machado/Getty Images; pp. 5, 16 Jose Breton- Pics Action/Shutterstock.com; p. 6 Robert Beck/Sports Illustrated via Getty Images; p. 7 Brian Bahr/Getty Images; p. 9 EMPICS Sport - PA Images via Getty Images; p. 11 Joe Petro/Icon Sportswire via Getty Images; p. 13 (main) Action Foto Sport/NurPhoto via Getty Images; p. 13 (inset) Taylor Ballantyne/Sports Illustrated/Getty Images; p. 15 (main) Kevin C. Cox/Getty Images; p. 15 (inset) Ira L. Black/Corbis via Getty Images; p. 17 Marc Atkins/Getty Images; p. 18 Franck Fife/AFP via Getty Images; p. 21 T.Sumaetho/Shutterstock.com.

Library of Congress Cataloging-in-Publication Data

Names: Kawa, Katie, author.
Title: Megan Rapinoe : making a difference as an athlete / Katie Kawa.
Description: First edition. | New York : KidHaven Publishing, 2021. |
    Series: People who make a difference | Includes bibliographical
    references and index.
Identifiers: LCCN 2019056345 (print) | LCCN 2019056346 (ebook) | ISBN
    9781534534742 (library binding) | ISBN 9781534534728 (paperback) | ISBN
    9781534534735 (set) | ISBN 9781534534759 (ebook)
Subjects: LCSH: Rapinoe, Megan, 1985—Juvenile literature. | Women soccer
    players–United States–Biography–Juvenile literature. | Soccer
    players–United States–Biography–Juvenile literature. | Political
    activists–United States–Biography–Juvenile literature.
Classification: LCC GV942.7.R366 K39 2021 (print) | LCC GV942.7.R366
    (ebook) | DDC 796.334092 2–dc23
LC record available at https://lccn.loc.gov/2019056345
LC ebook record available at https://lccn.loc.gov/2019056346

Printed in the United States of America

Some of the images in this book illustrate individuals who are models. The depictions do not imply actual situations or events.

CPSIA compliance information: Batch #BS20K: For further information contact Greenhaven Publishing LLC, New York, New York at 1-844-317-7404.

Please visit our website, www.greenhavenpublishing.com. For a free color catalog of all our high-quality books, call toll free 1-844-317-7404 or fax 1-844-317-7405.

Find us on

CONTENTS

On and Off the Field 4

Family Matters 6

Soccer Successes 8

Playing Professionally 10

The Fight for Equal Pay 12

Speaking Out and Showing Support 14

The Best in the World 16

A Confident Captain 18

An Athlete and an Activist 20

Glossary 22

For More Information 23

Index 24

ON AND OFF THE FIELD

Many athletes—people who play sports—make a difference on the field. They make big plays that help their teams win important games. However, some athletes also make a difference off the field. They know they have fans who listen when they talk. They use that **platform** to call attention to important issues and to inspire their fans. This means they move their fans to do great things.

Megan Rapinoe is an athlete who's made a big difference on the field and off of it. She's a soccer superstar who fights for equal rights and equal pay. Just by being herself, she inspires people around the world!

In Her Words

"Caring is cool. Lending your platform to others is cool. Sharing your knowledge and your success ... and your power is cool."

— *Glamour* magazine Women of the Year Awards speech from November 2019

Megan Rapinoe was one of the stars of the United States Women's National Team (USWNT) that won the FIFA Women's World Cup in 2015 and 2019. The World Cup is the most important soccer tournament, or set of matches, a country can win.

FAMILY MATTERS

Megan was born on July 5, 1985. She grew up in Redding, California, and loved to play outside, especially with her twin sister, Rachael. In fact, Megan and Rachael played soccer together in college for the University of Portland. Doing well in school was important to them too.

Megan hurt her knee in college, and she had to work hard to keep playing. However, she didn't give up. She wanted to be like the members of the USWNT that won the World Cup in 1999. That team inspired her—and many young soccer players—to be the best they could be!

1999 USWNT

In Her Words

"Two things really helped me survive [get through] middle school: Sports and my sister."

— "You Can't Get Rid of Your Girl That Easily," written for *The Players' Tribune* on June 23, 2019

Family is very important to Megan and to the other members of the USWNT. Megan is shown here with her mom in 2015.

SOCCER SUCCESSES

Soon, Megan would be just like the women she looked up to on the 1999 USWNT. Fans first noticed her during the 2011 World Cup, when her passing skills helped her team in big games. Although the USWNT lost the World Cup that year, they went on to win the World Cup in 2015. Megan scored two goals in the 2015 tournament.

Megan has also been part of teams that played in the Olympics. In 2012, she scored three goals at the Summer Olympics in London, England. The United States took home the gold medal—the top prize—at those Olympics.

In Her Words

"We don't just pop up once every four years on your TV, ready to win the World Cup. It's a constant, neverending grind, even without the actual soccer part. But! It's also the coolest job in the world."

— "You Can't Get Rid of Your Girl That Easily," written for *The Players' Tribune* on June 23, 2019

Megan likes to have fun on the field! She's become known for the way she **celebrates** during and after big games.

PLAYING PROFESSIONALLY

Megan also plays soccer professionally, which means she gets paid to play the sport as her job. In the United States, the National Women's Soccer League (NWSL) is the professional league, or group of teams, for women's soccer. Megan has become an important part of the NWSL.

Megan began playing for Seattle Reign FC, which is now known as Reign FC, in 2013. In 2018, she became the club's all-time leading scorer. The next year, she was honored as a Reign FC Legend. This honor is given to women who've made a difference in the Seattle, Washington, area and around the world.

In Her Words

"I think we learn from a very young age that it's okay to be **confident** and okay to take up that much space. It's okay to be bold and be big in those moments. As a team, we act that way and hold ourselves that way. I think, individually, we all gain confidence from that."

— Interview with Reign FC from July 2019

Megan has played as both a forward and a midfielder. A forward tries to score goals and often plays closest to the other team's goal. A midfielder plays in the middle of the field and often tries to help their teammates score goals.

THE FIGHT FOR EQUAL PAY

Megan and her teammates get paid to play soccer. However, throughout the history of soccer, women have been paid much less than men are to play the sport they love. Megan and the rest of the USWNT felt this was unfair, especially because their team had been more successful than the U.S. men's soccer team.

In 2016, Megan and five of her teammates filed a **complaint** about their unequal pay. When that didn't fix the problem, they filed a lawsuit against the U.S. Soccer **Federation** in 2019. This means they were ready to go to court to fight for equal pay.

In Her Words

"The **conversation** is no longer about should we have equal pay, or should we be supporting women. It's how do we support not only athletes but women in general."

— Interview with *TIME* magazine from July 2019

#EQUAL PAY
FOR EQUAL PLAY

By speaking out about the fight for equal pay in soccer, Megan and her teammates made fans aware of this problem. In fact, after the USWNT won the World Cup in 2019, fans in the stands began saying, "Equal pay! Equal pay!"

13

SPEAKING OUT AND SHOWING SUPPORT

Equal pay for women isn't the only issue Megan has spoken out about. She's a proud member of the **LGBT+** community who fights for equal rights for all people. People look up to her because she's open about who she is and who she loves.

Megan has also called attention to racism. She joined professional football player Colin Kaepernick and other athletes in kneeling during the U.S. national **anthem**. They did this to **protest** what they saw as the unfair way African Americans are treated. Some people felt Megan was being disrespectful, but she felt she was doing the right thing.

In Her Words

"It's important to have white people stand in support of people of color on this. We don't need to be the leading voice, of course, but standing in support of them is something that's really powerful."

— Interview from September 2016, after she began kneeling during the national anthem

In 2017, U.S. Soccer made a rule that all players had to stand during the national anthem. Megan followed this rule but chose not to sing or put her hand over her heart. Many people have strong feelings about her actions during the national anthem. Some people support her, but others feel she should protest in a different way.

THE BEST IN THE WORLD

In 2019, Megan's voice became even more powerful when the USWNT won the World Cup in France. Megan was one of the captains, or leaders, of the USWNT. She scored six goals in the World Cup, which earned her the Golden Boot as the tournament's leading scorer. She also won the Golden Ball, which is given to the best player at the World Cup.

Megan and her teammates became superstars after their World Cup win. They used their platform to talk about equal pay, LGBT+ issues, and women's rights. They wanted to use their time in the spotlight to inspire people, especially young girls.

In Her Words

"I hope we look back and think that this World Cup helped change the world for the better."

— Interview with Reign FC from July 2019

Megan won many awards at the World Cup and after it, including FIFA's The Best award, which is an honor given to the world's best female soccer player.

A CONFIDENT CAPTAIN

Throughout history, women were often made to feel like they couldn't be openly confident or proud of their talents. Megan and her teammates fought back against this idea by being the best in the world—and proud of it.

When Megan scored at the 2019 World Cup, she celebrated by spreading her arms wide. Many people saw this pose as a sign of her confidence, and it inspired women and LGBT+ people around the world to be more confident too. Megan is a strong woman who isn't afraid to show her true self. She makes others feel like they can also be proud of who they are!

In Her Words

"You will not silence us, you will not take the smile off our face, you will not take anything from us. We're coming. We're here. We're not leaving."

— Interview with *TIME* magazine from July 2019 about what her goal celebration meant

The Life of
Megan Rapinoe

1985
Megan Rapinoe is born on July 5.

2005
Megan and her twin sister, Rachael, win a college soccer championship with the University of Portland.

2011
Megan plays in the FIFA Women's World Cup in Germany.

2012
Megan wins a gold medal at the Olympics in London.

2013
Megan beings playing professional soccer in Seattle.

2015
Megan is part of the USWNT that wins the World Cup in Canada.

2016
Megan and her teammates file a complaint about unequal pay.

Megan plays on the U.S. Olympic team in Rio de Janeiro, Brazil.

2018
Megan becomes the all-time leading scorer for Reign FC.

2019
Megan is part of an equal pay lawsuit against U.S. Soccer.

The USWNT wins the World Cup in France.

Megan wins the Golden Ball, Golden Boot, and FIFA The Best awards.

Megan's soccer successes show that she and her teammates have many reasons to be proud of themselves!

AN ATHLETE AND AN ACTIVIST

Athletes are often **role model**s for young people. Megan Rapinoe knows this because she had her own sports heroes as a girl—the 1999 USWNT. They inspired her to believe that girls could become sports superstars. Now, she and her teammates know it's their job to inspire a new **generation** of young athletes.

Megan hosts soccer camps where she teaches kids about sports and life. She also uses **social media** to raise awareness about causes she cares about. She makes a difference in many ways as both an athlete and an activist—a person who's working to change the world for the better.

In Her Words

"This is my charge to everyone. We have to be better … We have to love more, hate less. We've got to listen more and talk less. We've got to know that … it's our **responsibility** to make this world a better place."

— Speech after the 2019 World Cup victory parade in New York City

Be Like Megan Rapinoe!

If you see someone being treated unfairly, help them, and tell a trusted adult.

Treat everyone fairly.

Believe in yourself, and remind your friends to believe in themselves.

Work hard in school and in your after-school activities, such as sports or music lessons.

Speak or write about issues that matter to you.

Be active, and inspire your friends to be active too.

You don't have to be a famous athlete to make a difference in the world around you. These are just some ideas for how you can get started!

GLOSSARY

anthem: A song that honors a country.

celebrate: To do something special to honor an important event or accomplishment.

complaint: A formal statement that someone is unhappy about something.

confident: Having a feeling of belief that you can do something well, which is also known as confidence.

conversation: The act of talking.

federation: A group that is made by joining other groups together.

generation: A group of people born and living during the same time.

LGBT+: Relating to a group made up of people who see themselves as a gender different from the sex they were assigned at birth or who want to be in romantic relationships that aren't only male-female. LGBT stands for lesbian, gay, bisexual, and transgender.

platform: A place or opportunity for public discussion.

protest: To speak out strongly against something.

responsibility: A duty that a person should do.

role model: A person whose behavior is imitated by others.

social media: A collection of websites and applications, or apps, that allow users to interact with each other and create online communities.

FOR MORE INFORMATION

WEBSITES

ESPN: Megan Rapinoe

www.espn.com/soccer/player/_/id/158775/megan-rapinoe

ESPN's Megan Rapinoe page has facts about her games for Reign FC and the USWNT, news stories, and videos.

We Are Rapinoe

www.rapinoe.us/about/

This official website features facts about Megan and Rachael Rapinoe, as well as causes they care about.

BOOKS

Jökulsson, Illugi. *Stars of Women's Soccer*. New York, NY: Abbeville Press, 2018.

Kortemeier, Todd. *Make Me the Best Soccer Player*. Minneapolis, MN: ABDO Publishing, 2017.

Sherman, Jill. *Megan Rapinoe*. Mankato, MN: Amicus Publishing, 2020.

INDEX

A

awards, 4, 17, 19

C

college, 6, 19

E

equal pay, 4, 12, 13, 14, 16, 19

G

goals, 8, 11, 16, 18

H

honors, 10, 17

K

Kaepernick, Colin, 14

L

lawsuits, 12, 19
LGBT+ community, 14, 16, 18

N

national anthem, 14, 15
National Women's Soccer League (NWSL), 10

O

Olympics, 8, 19

R

racism, 14
Rapinoe, Rachael, 6, 19

S

Seattle Reign FC, 10, 16, 19
social media, 20

T

teammates, 11, 12, 13, 16, 18, 19, 20

U

United States Women's National Team (USWNT), 5, 6, 7, 8, 12, 13, 16, 19, 20
U.S. Soccer Federation, 12

W

women, 10, 12, 14, 16, 18
World Cup, 5, 6, 8, 13, 16, 17, 18, 19, 20